Combat Helicopters

by Jay Schleifer

Capstone Press
MINNEAPOLIS

Printed in the United States of America.

Capstone Press • 2440 Fernbrook Lane • Minneapolis, MN 55447

Editorial Director John Coughlan
Managing Editor Tom Streissguth
Production Editor James Stapleton
Book Design Tim Halldin

Library of Congress Cataloging-in-Publication Data

Schleifer, Jay.
Combat helicopters / Jay Schleifer.
p. cm. -- (Wings)
Includes bibliographical references and index.
Summary: Presents a history of military helicopters with descriptions of some notable models from the U.S. Air Force.
ISBN 1-56065-305-1 : $13.35
1. Military helicopters--Juvenile literature. [1. Military helicopters. 2. Helicopters.] I. Title. II. Series: Wings (Minneapolis, Minn.)
UG1230.S35 1996
355.83--dc20

95-11247
CIP
AC

Table of Contents

AH-64D
LONGBOW

Chapter 1

Helicopter War

The time was the 1960s, and the place was Vietnam. U.S. forces were fighting against Viet Cong guerrillas, who moved and attacked in small bands. From their bases, the guerrillas staged hit-and-run raids on U.S. camps and ammunition dumps.

At one mountaintop hideout, the guerrillas felt safe. Steep cliffs protected them on all sides. The only danger of attack was from the sky.

A combat helicopter takes a steep dive during a flight test.

An Apache helicopter flies over hot and dusty desert terrain during the Gulf War of 1991.

One day, a frightening sound came from the sky. Waves of Hueys–long, green helicopters–rose from behind the trees.

The first choppers were heavily armed **gunships** that forced the guerrillas to take cover. Moments later, **troop carriers** arrived.

Infantry soldiers slid down rope ladders that hung from the helicopter doors. Larger choppers carrying supplies flew over, along with air ambulances to take out the wounded. A whole army was moving in.

The guerrillas quickly began waving a white flag. In a matter of minutes, the battle was over–and the Hueys had won it.

Chapter 2

A New Kind of Flying and Fighting Machine

Of all the world's aircaft types, the helicopter is the newest. The first workable models were flown in the late 1930s by a Russian inventor named Igor Sikorsky. The company he started, Sikorsky Aircraft, still builds helicopters today.

As soon as military leaders saw Sikorsky's invention, they began thinking of ways to use it in battle. Helicopters could take off and land anywhere. They could fly an entire army right

The Cobra helicopter gunship is a fast and effective weapon in air-to-ground combat.

The Sikorsky VS-300 was an early experimental helicopter.

over the heads of the strongest enemy defenses and land on top of enemy headquarters. Choppers could take troops from one battleground to the next. Helicopters could hit and run and get away to do it again, just like the **cavalry** soldiers of earlier wars. Helos would be an air cavalry.

The armies of several nations flew experimental helicopters through the 1940s. No helicopter saw battle in World War II. But the new machines did see action during the Korean War (1950-53). In the 1960s, the U.S. Army

The early Sikorsky choppers were not as well armed as modern aircraft.

tried its choppers in the Vietnam War. So many flew that this conflict was known as "The Helicopter War."

World War II produced a great fighter in the Mustang and a great bomber in the B-29. But it was the Vietnam War that produced the first great combat helicopter–the Bell Huey.

The Sikorsky SR-5 had seats for two passengers in the glass-covered nose.

Bell UH-1 Iroquois ("Huey")

If you live near an army base, you've probably seen a tadpole-shaped helicopter that makes a whump-whump sound as it passes overhead. That's the Huey, the first modern combat helicopter.

Before the Huey, most army helicopters looked like a fishbowl hooked to a fishing pole. Without wings, they needed more power than airplanes of their size just to get off the ground. That meant carrying a huge piston engine that took up most of the room on board.

These big engines made easy targets. Often the enemy didn't need to shoot friendly helicopters down to keep them out of action. Early choppers had cables, gears, belts, and other moving parts. For every hour in the air, they spent days under repair in the hanger.

The new craft could carry messages, watch the enemy from on high, and carry the wounded away. But flying them into battle was impossible.

The tadpole-shaped Huey was a common sight for U.S. troops during the Vietnam War.

The Jet Age

Then, in the 1950s, the jet age came along. A special jet engine called a **turboshaft** was built for helicopters. The engine's hot exhaust turned a windmill-like device called a turbine. The turbine spun the **rotors**–the blades that lifted and balanced the helicopter.

628
679

Jet engines were smaller than piston engines, yet more powerful. They had fewer parts that could break down. Designers couldn't wait to try them on the helicopter.

Bell Aircraft of Texas was one of the first companies to produce a jet-powered craft. The 1,400-horsepower engine sat over the cabin instead of filling up the body. This left plenty of room for troops or cargo. The slim, 57-foot (17.4-meter) machine could cruise at 125 miles (201 kilometers) per hour. It had a range of 280 miles (451 kilometers).

The U.S. Army nicknames its choppers after Native American tribes. Bell's new bird was called the Iroquois, after a tribe that lives in the northeastern United States and Canada. But before long, soldiers began calling it the "Huey" after its first model number, HU-1. (The model number is now UH-1).

Hueys practice air assaults during infantry training.

Hueys flew everywhere in Vietnam. They ferried in the first U.S. soldiers to arrive in the early 1960s. And a Huey airlifted the last troops out in 1974.

In between, Hueys carried troops and cargo. They saved wounded troops by getting them to hospitals faster than a ground ambulance could. And the U.S. lost more HU-1s than any other kind of aircraft. More than 5,000 Hueys never came back from Vietnam.

Early in the war, the Huey learned to fight. Crews began fitting their birds with rocket packs and machine guns. The armed helos would clear a patch of jungle before the troop-carriers went in. This was the first use of the helicopter gunship.

In the late 1960s, a special Huey was built just for the job of clearing enemy strongholds. It was narrower, faster, and better armed than cargo-carrying models. The crew of two sat one behind the other, as in a fighter jet. The new bird's twin guns could fire thousands of shots a minute.

This was the AH-1 Huey Cobra gunship. The Cobras could overpower an enemy force on the ground. Some even shot down enemy jet fighters. More than 2,700 Cobras are still in military use today.

The Huey and the Cobra have been used by the army, navy, air force and Marine Corps. Canadian forces have also used them. During the Vietnam War, even the enemy flew captured Hueys.

The fast and well-armed Cobra can fire several thousand rounds a minute.

Chapter 3

The Sub Hunters

It's as silent as a shark, and much more dangerous. In fact, the submarine may be the most dangerous warship ever built.

Running underwater, subs can sneak up to within a few miles of a target nation. They can stand by for months at a time, waiting for an order to fire. If war comes, one sub can fire up to 20 **nuclear**-armed missiles. These weapons could destroy entire cities with almost no warning.

While carrying heavy cargo, a pair of Sikorsky Sea Stallions refuel in mid-flight.

The armed forces of the major nations hunt these killer subs every day, and around the clock. This kind of mission is known as **ASW (anti-submarine warfare)**. In peacetime, the subs' hiding spots are recorded on a map. But if a war broke out, the subs would be among the first targets of an attack.

No weapon is more important to sub hunting than the helicopter. And no helo is better at it than the Kaman SH-2 Seasprite.

Kaman SH-2 Seasprite

The SH-2 Seasprite is just 40 feet (12.2 meters) long–17 feet (5.2 meters) shorter than a Huey. The Seasprite can fit on board the small, fast **destroyers** that the navy uses in anti-submarine warfare.

These ships do an ocean version of guard duty. By trailing long wires with microphones, they can listen for the deep rumble of a submarine. The destroyers may also use a sub-hunting system called **sonar**. Sonar sends out a sound–usually a loud "PING"–through the

When based on destroyers, Seasprites can carry out a variety of missions at sea.

water. The sound bounces back as an echo when it strikes a submarine ("PING...ping"). The stronger the bounceback, the closer the sub. When the destroyer's sonar finds a sub, the Seasprite goes to work.

Powered by two 1,307-horsepower jet engines, the SH-2 can fly at 150 miles (241 kilometers) per hour. It drops portable sonar sets, called **sonobuoys**, into the water to find its undersea target. Seasprites also use powerful magnetic sensors to detect large metal objects under the surface. If a **periscope** pops out of the waves, the crew of the SH-2 will see it on their radar.

While facing an ASW helo, a sub captain will try to hide by shutting down his engines and all other systems. But a Seasprite can

The heavy Sea Stallion is useful for cargo transport as well as sea patrol work.

hover over a sub for two and a half hours. If the submarine hasn't moved by then, a second helicopter will arrive to keep it pinned down.

To attack the submarine, the Seasprite can drop **smart bombs** or **torpedos**. These weapons start tracking the sub as soon as they hit the water. They close in at high speed for the kill.

The latest SH-2s carry the Navy's **LAMPS** multi-mission packages. This equipment allows the Seasprite to track submarines, attack surface ships, carry out **SAR** (search-and-rescue) work, and transport cargo as well.

Other oceangoing helicopters include the Russian Kamov series, the Sikorsky Sea Stallion, and the British Navy Lynx. When a sub captain sees any one of these overhead, he knows he's in deep trouble.

Chapter 4

Russian Helicopters

The first workable combat helicopters flew just after World War II. At the same time, the U.S., England, Canada, and other nations were in a Cold War with Russia (then part of the Soviet Union). Although there was no fighting, Russian combat helicopters were facing the U.S. and its allies in Europe.

The Russians are among the world's best helicopter builders. Most of their machines come from two makers, Kamov and Mil. Many

The Soviet Mi-24 Hind takes aim with four machine-gun pods.

Kamovs carry twin rotors. The rotors, which are the same size, spin in opposite directions to balance each other. Like Seasprites, Kamovs often fly from ships for ASW work.

Mil helicopters are big, single-rotor craft. They're the world champions at helicopter weightlifting. A Mil can lift more than 25,000 pounds (11,340 kilograms), the weight of a six-wheel army truck. One experimental model carried 88,000 pounds (39,917 kilograms) more than a mile into the sky.

Kamovs carry two rotors, equal in size, to balance the chopper in flight.

U.S. experts give Russian helos nicknames that begin with "H." Russian pilots may not mind flying a "Halo," "Hip," or "Haze." They may be less happy with the names "Hog" and "Hoodlum." The best-known of all Russian choppers, though, may be the Mil-24 "Hind."

Russian Mil-24 Hind

In the 1960s, the U.S. entered the Vietnam War. There was a need for a fast, tough helo–the Huey–that could fight in rugged terrain. In the 1970s, Russia fought a guerrilla war in the Asian country of Afghanistan. The helicopter of that war was the Mil-24 Hind.

The Hind is the same length as a Huey–57 feet (17.4 meters). But it has a bigger, 56-foot (17.1-meter) rotor with five blades, instead of two. With twin engines of 2,300 horsepower each, the Mil has three times the power of a Huey and a top speed of 190 miles (306 kilometers) per hour. Its range is 466 miles (750 kilometers).

Like the Huey, the first Mil was a cargo carrier. Later versions carried arms and ammunition. The best-known Mil gunship is the Mi-24D. It can carry 80 rockets, two machine guns, air-to-ground missiles, and 3,000 pounds (1,361 kilograms) of bombs.

The Mi-24D can carry machine guns, missiles, rockets, and bombs.

Many of the weapons sit under the chopper's **miniwings**. These two small side wings help lift the copter in flight. There's also a fast-firing cannon in the nose.

There's less chance now that the U.S. and Russia will ever meet in battle. But the brutal looking Mil is still one of the most feared combat helicopters in the world.

Chapter 5

Future Copters

As helicopters go, the Huey and the Mil-24 are great machines. But they are also machines of the past. They carry guns and rockets–the kind of weapons used in World War II. Night or fog blind them, and snow or heavy rain will keep them on the ground.

Tomorrow's wars will be fought day and night, in all kinds of weather. Computers and **lasers** will be as important as guns. The army of the future needs helicopters that can handle these new challenges.

The Apache carries a complex radar system on top of its rotor.

Several such future copters are already flying for the U.S. Army. Here are three of them.

Sikorsky UH-60 Blackhawk

The chopper that replaced the Huey as the army's all-purpose chopper is the Blackhawk. This 64-foot-long, flat-topped chopper holds 11 fully armed troops. Its twin 2,828-horsepower engines drive it as fast as 150 miles (241

The Blackhawk lifts an infantry team into a combat zone during field exercises.

kilometers) per hour. It packs easily into the air force's cargo planes, so it can quickly get to battle zones anywhere in the world.

There are many different types of Hawks. The Nighthawk, a night flyer, is useful for search-and-rescue missions. The Seahawk helps the Navy with missions at sea. The Pave-Hawk gunship is named for the Pave-Low tracking system. This equipment can follow the enemy by detecting body heat. There's even a peacetime Hawk: the VH-60A model. This is

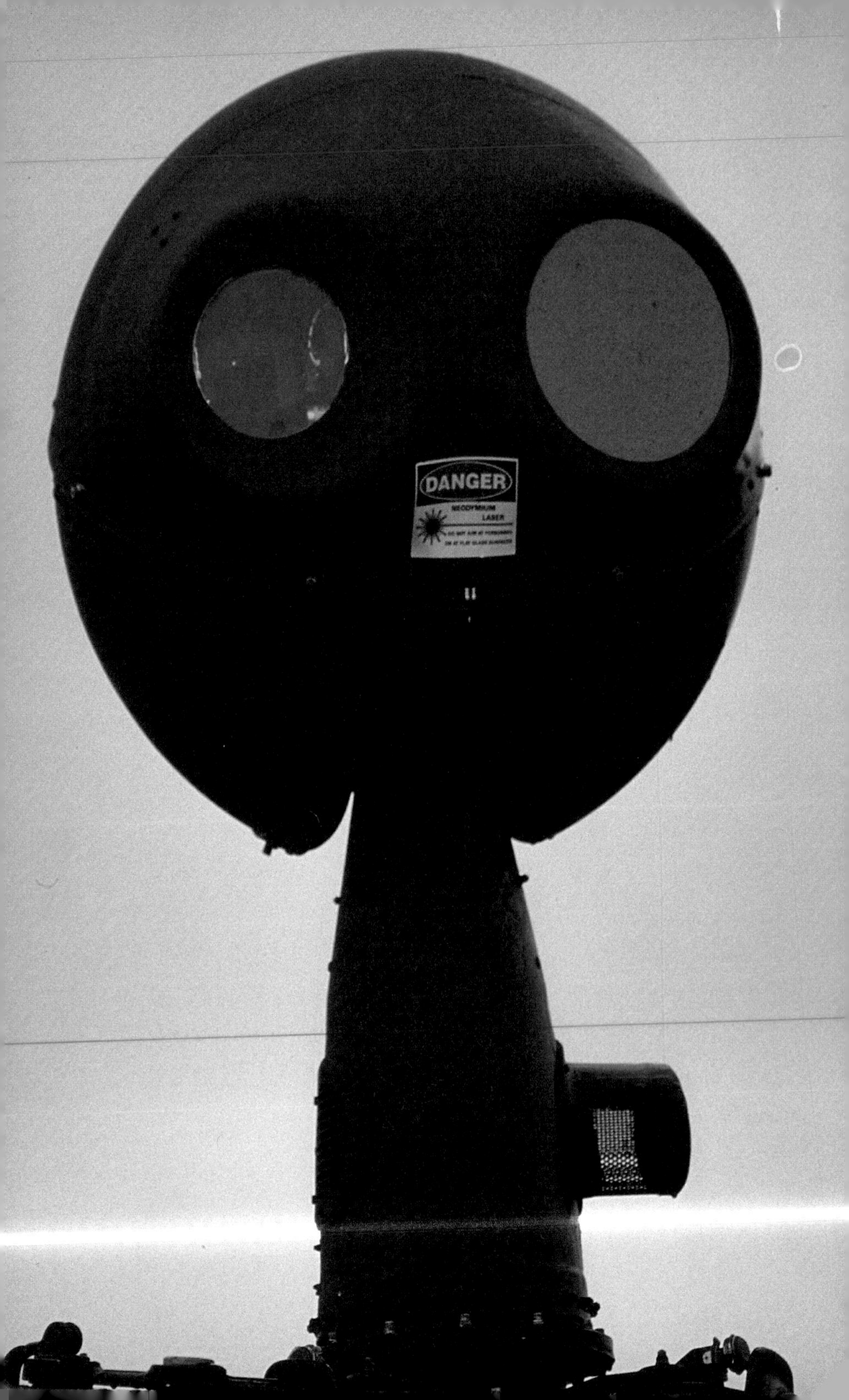
DANGER
LASER

the personal helicopter of U.S. leaders, including the president.

There are more than 2,000 Hawk choppers in use, and probably 2,000 different ways they are being used.

Bell OH-58D Kiowa

This 42-foot (12.8-meter) -long, 65-horsepower scout helicopter looks like the Bell JetRanger chopper, which traffic spotters fly. But peacetime Bells don't carry the Kiowa's strange-looking "bugeye" ball, which sits over the main rotor. The Kiowa uses this system to do traffic spotting on a battlefield.

The ball holds television and heat-detecting "eyes" that spot targets. Their position above the rotor lets the chopper sneak up on an enemy camp from below the treetops. The Kiowa can float just high enough for the twin eyes to see over the trees.

The bugeye ball in the Kiowa can "see" heat as well as enemy movement.

The pictures show on screens in the Kiowa's cockpit. There are also five different radios to report the enemy's location to headquarters and call in the gunships.

Kiowas can also fly **NOE** (nap of the earth). They can rocket along just a few feet off the ground at up to 125 miles (201 kilometers) per hour. They rise and descend to follow the landscape. Radar can't see them at this low height. Any enemy soldier who does might be

The Kiowa is armed with machine guns and rockets.

The Apache can fly in all kinds of weather and under dangerous conditions.

so startled by this low-flying craft that he doesn't report anything.

McDonnell-Douglas AH-64 Apache

No Native American tribe fought more skillfully than the Apache of the southwest. That's also true of the amazing gunship that

carries their name. Some call it the most awesome combat helicopter of them all.

The AH-64 flies like no other chopper. Its twin 1,690-horsepower engines drive this 48-foot (14.6-meter) warrior to speeds of over 200 miles (322 kilometers) per hour. It can fly day or night, in any weather. Special systems use heat from the earth to create a television picture of the landscape. In the cockpit, the pilot can see where he's going even in a heavy fog.

The Apache is armed with the Hellfire laser-following missile. To fire, the gunner lights the target with a beam of laser light. The missile rides the beam for up to five miles to the target.

The Apache can track several targets at once. It carries fast-firing guns that the gunner can aim through a special helmet gunsight. He aims the missiles just by turning his head.

The Apache's Hellfire missiles use a beam of light to find their way to the target.

The Apache is an especially safe helicopter for the crew. Each of the two fliers has a separate armored cockpit. If one pilot takes a direct hit from enemy fire, the other will survive. This feature makes the Apache one of the most popular combat helicopters among pilots.

The Apache also gets the attention of its opponents. During the Gulf War of 1991, when the U.S. fought Iraq, one Apache made a single pass against an enemy camp. Dozens of Iraqis instantly ran out waving white flags. Without firing a shot, they had surrendered just from the sight of it.

The Apache is the most advanced model in the long line of combat helicopters.

Glossary

ASW (anti-submarine warfare)–methods used to hunt down and sink submarines. These include tracking the subs by sound, using magnetic devices that can detect metal, and radar.

cavalry–troops of soldiers on horseback. They moved quickly from place to place on the battlefield and carried out hit-and-run attacks on the enemy.

destroyer–a small, fast warship used to hunt submarines

gunship–an armed helicopter

hover–to hang in mid-air

LAMPS–equipment that gives anti-submarine helicopters the ability to carry out other missions while fighting submarines

laser–a device that produces a straight beam of light energy, used to aim or track weapons

miniwings–stub wings on helicopters used for extra lift and as mounts for weapons

NOE–nap-of-the-earth flying, in which the pilot flies just above ground level. This kind of flying can help a helicopter to hide from radar.

nuclear–a weapon that uses atomic power, the same power that heats the sun

periscope–a viewing tube that a submarine crew uses to see objects and ships on the surface

rotor–a propeller-like device on a helicopter. The main rotor provides lift and forward speed. The tail rotor is used for balance and steering.

SAR–search and rescue

smart bomb–a bomb that can be steered as it falls, either by radio or through a long wire that unrolls from the aircraft that dropped it

sonar–a method of tracking submarines by using sounds and echos

sonobuoy–a portable sonar device dropped or trailed by helicopter

torpedo–a self-propelled water weapon that explodes on contact with a ship or submarine

troop carrier–a helicopter designed to carry soldiers into battle

turboshaft–a helicopter engine that uses jet exhaust to turn a turbine wheel, which then spins the rotors

To Learn More

Baker, Dr. David. *Helicopters.* Vero Beach, Florida: Rourke Publishing Group, 1989.

Scutts, Jerry. *Combat Helicopters.* New York: Mallard Press, 1989.

Stapfer, Hans-Heiri. *Soviet Military Helicopters.* London: Arms and Armour Press, 1991.

Sullivan, George. *Military Aircraft: Modern Combat Helicopters.* New York: Facts on File, 1993.

Photo credits: Air Force Association: p. 24; Bell Helicopter-Textron: pp. 13, 17, 36; Don Berliner: p. 26; Dept. of Defense: pp. 21, 32, 33; ©William B. Folsom: pp. 8, 14, 34; Paul Jackson: pp. 28-29; McDonnell Douglas: pp. 4, 6-7, 30, 37, 38, 40, 41; Sikorsky Aircraft: pp. 10, 11 (top and bottom), 18, 22.

Some Useful Addresses

National Air and Space Museum
6th Street and Independence Avenue
Washington, DC 20560

United States Air Force Museum
Wright-Patterson Air Force Base, OH 45433

New England Air Museum
Bradley International Airport
Windsor Locks, CT 06096

National Aviation Museum
P.O. Box 9724
Ottawa, Ontario KIG 543

Index